A Year Without a Season:
Poems from the Miami Valley

Also by Jacquelyn Merrill Ruiz

Poetry
The Fish, The Twins, The Ram
The White Stairs
The Swan

Non-fiction
Swedes in Lowell

A Year Without a Season:
Poems from the Miami Valley

Jacquelyn Merrill Ruiz

Spear Stone Press
Cincinnati

A Year Without A Season: Poems from the Miami Valley

Copyright © 2024 by Jacquelyn Merrill Ruiz

www.jmerrillruiz.com

All rights reserved. No part of this book may be reproduced or transmitted in any form or by any means, or by any information storage and retrieval system without the written permission of the publisher, except where permitted by law.

Printed in the United States of America.
First Edition

Book design by Jacquelyn Merrill Ruiz
Cover by Jacquelyn Merrill Ruiz, with Canva

ISBN 978-0-9963034-6-0
LCCN 2024913101

Spear Stone Press
Cincinnati
www.spearstonepress.com

*For all the cats who saw me through 2020:
Poopsmith, Witch Baby, Sage, Murray, Ruka, Midnight, Morgana,
Kahlua, Aja, Sherlock, Tempest, Boone, Echo, MooMoo, Shinobu,
Phedre, Joscelin, Mina, and MiniMoo;
for all the cats I knew before 2020;
and for all the cats I knew after.*

Contents

The Year Dawns	11
I Could Never Wear a Watch	12
Boone Hunts	13
A starling watches	15
Scrying by Cat Belly	17
I Dream of Sleeping, Unless I Dream of Eating	18
Ode to Negative Eight	19
Phoebe, sleeping curled	21
Aja Finds Her Soulmate	23
It Could be Affection, It Could be Hunger	24
I put my day together	25
The Darkest Timeline	26
An Ode to Witch Baby	27
An Ode to Poopsmith	28
The Window, the Want	29
Rewilding	30
I saw a great bush of yellow flowers blooming	31
How to Get Me Out of Bed	32
Painted in art deco	35
Spring's Already Too Late to Trim the Roses	37
Certainty is Soft, but Ask Anyway	38
When the kittens were newborn	39
Mockingbird waits; silence	41
Always Testing My Boundaries	43
Entryway	44
A goldfinch is back	45
Orange tabby deep in dreams	47
Family Resemblance	49
Sometimes Fate Requires Two Hands	50
Gift of the Birch	51
Chipmunks and grackles	53
Birds Hate Mondays Too	55
Queen Tempest	56
Fourteen sparrows dig	59
Why Science When I Can Astrology?	61

Lessons After Death	62
Today is gentle	63
Snowing pear blossoms	65
For another year	67
The First Aid Kit is Missing	69
Sanctuary in Wood, in Paper	70
The seasons turned. I felt the pop	73
Doctor Boone	75
Leaves flip light-side-up	77
One Reason to Befriend Animals	79
Two Scouts	80
Giant, velvet slug	83
Echo's purr is a growl	85
Theme Song Changes Suddenly	87
Tea leaves whisper my fate	89
When the Only Sounds are Birds, Everything Becomes a Bird	91
Moths are so polite	92
At the Bottom	93
Society Turns Me Away and I'm Back to Playing in the Dirt	94
The World Ended While My Neighbor Mowed His Lawn	95
It Is Too Goddamn Hot	96
Increase the heat	97
Evolution Through Excision	98
A Surprising Case of Self-Protection	99
We were always going to destroy ourselves	100
Ambition but Unknown	101
Trust Folly	102
The Climate Changed but I Can't	103
Supplanter	104
My Alarm Clock is the Kind That Wakes You Up with a Gradual Dawning and Nature Sounds	105
Voting Isn't Enough. I Have to [REDACTED]	106
Grackles	107
Chasing Mourning Doves	108
Inside Again	109
The seasons are lost to me	110
Empires Fall	111

This is not a poem	112
Silence is a Lie	113
Bitter Fruit	114
Halloween 2020	115
More Like "Daylight LOSING Time"	116
Before the Birds Awake	117
Witness	118
Selenite	119
Tell Them I'm Fine	120
The Season of Murder Mysteries	121
The Shrinking Forest	122
I Only Have One Regret but Holding It Is A Full-Time Job	123
Is this our winter now	124
I kept my soul in a pocket watch	125
Bold of Me to Buy a Planner for the Upcoming Year	126
The Heart	127
Resolutions for the New Year	128
Maybe It'll End After All	129
Winter At Last	130
About the Author	133

The Year Dawns

A January afternoon, dull and crisp,
that perfect shade of dove gray—
a swatch of sky my mood ring,
thermometer, quick test to tell
if I'll go out. If it's ready for me,
chilly and overcast. I need it muted
from the spike of heat, the sharp shadows,
everything known at every glance—
too much, too much detail, contrast.

How can anyone work in the light?

How can anyone survive
the scrutiny of the heavens
without the tempered cold,

without the static veil?

I Could Never Wear a Watch

Even before this year without time,
it was too slippery a concept for me to grasp.
Since childhood, the only two demarcations
I comprehended were
day or night?
and
warm or cold?
When to sleep and how to dress.
Watches confuse me still. I can't read
digital, those blocky digits
are unknowable in relation to my day.
I know numbers and their order but
can't translate it to a moment in time.
Analog is slightly better—
the positions of the hands
in relation to each other
correspond to where they've been and where they're going.
I can see their history.
I must bypass numbers completely
if I want to participate in society.

I wonder if I've stumbled upon a truth,
like when I was little and decreed
a color theory
I was never taught. Another concept
I never learned, but know, like justice
or how to fall in love all wrong.

Boone Hunts

The largest cat sniffs the air,
turning up his enormous whiskers
like the branches of a winter birch.
A whiff caught his attention—
something I can't smell, for once,
something common among a house
full of unchanged scents.

He abandons the trail
and remembers that weird thing
on the sink he likes to lick,
the bitter lavender bar
that leaves a film on his tongue.

A starling watches,
chilly coat flecked like snow.
A wary staring contest.

Scrying by Cat Belly

Was morning ever so still?
The quiet, slanted light—the walls
so sturdy? I don't remember peace
like this, but maybe memory always becomes soft—
solid in its prime, ripe, and time
being time, breaks it down so you, reaching,
squish your hand through it
like an old watermelon
or deer carcass.

It's easy to tell the future.
It will be, eventually, what the past
is now and a new one
leapfrogs further, carrying forward
hopes and leaving behind
an insubstantial past.

Tempest remembers where the sunbeam
will lie across the couch, shifts
her sleepy cat body into position,
waits.
It hits her toes first, little beans curling,
and crawls across her. All she does
is remain. If only
anything were so easy for me, a promise
of stillness, a steady
grip.

I Dream of Sleeping, Unless I Dream of Eating

How has my life gone so wrong—
or maybe so right—
that the best dream in a bunch
of vibrant euphony
is my slow and deliberate completion
of savoring a toasted sesame bagel
with cream cheese.

Ode to Negative Eight

At last, we hit upon that winter day
so cold few scents can pierce its clarity—
because our nose is frozen through, the way
constricted with an icy brevity.
Today, the wooden deck decides to knock
a helpless cannonball against the house,
its planks a frozen bomb, inviting dock—
an edge, the cats and me are poised to pounce.
The birds are still, conserving energy,
paused song a forecast of the day ahead
requiring mittens, scarves, a hat, hot tea,
a cozy hearth, or retreat back to bed.
I do not yearn for spring but morning chills
and quiet isolation winter wills.

Phoebe, sleeping curled
around the cool toilet base—
too much catnip, friend.

Aja Finds her Soulmate

Aja bathes behind my sneakers
with the tongue that cleans her butt
and paws that dig through poop,
licks cat-fingers and rubs them
over her closed eyes,
nuzzles my filthy shoes, sticks
her whole face
into their musty depths.

It Could be Affection, It Could be Hunger

I've read it's the salt on my skin
that Tempest licks.
Not to clean me like a mama cat
or show affection,
and I believed it for a second,
just until she came back
and curled up,
stared at me, and purred
without being pet.
She doesn't purr
when licking crumbs
off buttery toast.
Maybe love is saline.

* * *

I put my day together
one piece
at a time,
resting
between each task,
tasks big
and tasks
every adult person
completes in a day.

Doctor says it's
anxiety.
The real kind,
the hard stuff.
The one that
makes
motivation
between getting
out of bed
and brushing teeth
a few hours
or a lifetime.

Worry only
does me good
when I would be
pinched
or thrillingly
exposed.

The Darkest Timeline

A ferret fucked us over in 2016
when it curled against the live wires
of a particle accelerator.

This sounds like every science fiction parody
from the early 1990s—no wonder
it's so common now to read the phrases
darkest timeline
and *if I pitched this premise,
I'd be fired.*

But it happened, I swear,
some Swiss raccoon seeking shelter
or warmth or food or death
was all it took to break time
and humanity must suffer for it.

I wish only women
would be the ones to reprogram us,
after.

An Ode to Witch Baby

She stalks her prey from shadows deep and far,
a flash of golden eyes or speckled rump
the only glimpse of predator. Her roar
a mighty squeak. She's not afraid to dump
your coffee on the floor or steal your trash—
she jumps in bins for crumpled Post-it notes.
She runs from friendly, petting hands, but asks
politely for more treats, and rubs her coat—
the softest fur—against your legs and feet.
So silently she glides, and runs beside
her pack of giant, ragtag friends. Defeat
is foreign to her noble soul. She rides
the "cute" excuse, but really, she's a brat,
and gets away with more than other cats.

An Ode to Poopsmith

What tiny beast entwines around my feet?
What black and tawny hide resideth there?
A reaching paw, a nuzzled jaw—so sweet,
I'll lift you up so you can eat my hair.
Your goofy face, wide eyes set far too close,
looks up at me in utter innocence.
I coo at you in cat, you start to doze,
your kitten limbs now limp, no longer tense.
You fall off desks, walk into walls, and sleep
embracing toilet bowls. Your siblings rush
when you just keep your cool, a patience deep
with cat naivete, and never push.
You're dumb, for sure, and pretty, and my own.
I'm glad you chose me for your always-home.

The Window, the Want

The birds speak, and answer,
a family of them in the pussywillow,
thriving through the winter
while the rest of us starve.
I know the phrase but it isn't attention I crave,
it's touch, and call,
and answer
when I speak in the empty room.

The quiet doesn't hurt.

Not on its own.

My skin is not disturbed, not a ripple
or tremor, the texture
of a still lake. I can't speak
and make it dance. I can't shout
myself to pleasure.
Maybe, today, it's warm enough to rain.
Maybe today will be more satisfying
than an echo.

Rewilding

The starlings plump in crowns
of birch. I've never seen them in the maple.
Height, maybe, the preference. I've tried
to make this square a world they would have recognized
a dozen years ago, but it was before their time
and mine—a swollen swathe of farmland.
The first few years, we had snakes and mice. Skunks,
foxes, coyote, moles. So many deer.
A hawk chased a mourning dove
into the back window, a downy smear
across the screen.
Now we get a plastic glove. Chewed tennis ball.
The only life we attract
as distant as possible
from the industrial detritus
we accumulate.

* * *

I saw a great bush of yellow flowers blooming
on someone's Instagram post,
far away from these slow Miami Valley
buds, which have struggled against the cold
longer into the season.
Years ago, the temperature hit 90 on March 19—
technically still winter.
May starts Friday and it's been a lovely
weird 60-something for two months.
I heard bees at the pussy willow
weeks ago
but nothing since.

How to Get Me Out of Bed

A cat calls me from sleep,
wondering if I'm gone for good,
wondering if she's next, she's starving,
starving, how am I so cruel?
A claw-sheathed paw searches my face—
in case I'm awake, she wants me to know
she cries out of concern,
not for selfish reasons at all,
but after she smooshes her face
all over my face, she nips
my nose ring and tugs.

Painted in Art Deco,
blue jays clear their throats:
an ugly yell from art.

Spring's Already Too Late to Trim the Roses

One brittle rosebud, preserved
in bruise-purple, shrunk
and rasping. The rest
is withered leaves hanging
from wintered stalks, spotted,
or white like bird-picked bones
and dry as straw. Only the thorns
don't dull—diligent
and unwilling
access to their wards long dead.
I should have trimmed them back
before December, but always
life—another bloom, milkweed bugs—
it's as much about respect
as not wanting to get my hands dirty.

Certainty is Soft, but Ask Anyway

He brings her seeds, tiny ones
without names and shares and asks,
asks again then flies off,
and she sits but doesn't wait.
She's not waiting, she just knows
he'll be back, and puffs her chest
and looks around deep
in these branches dense with green.
He returns and leaves, shy,
like a man carrying a ring
for weeks, waiting for the moment
it's right to ask and share,
his secret in his pocket, in his chest,
alive with certainty and fear.

* * *

When the kittens were newborn,
we fed them kibble and fish
and they made more cat out of it.

Cat from fish.

There's your alchemy.

Mockingbird waits; silence.
"Let me fill up this bored night
with each song I've learned!"

Always Testing My Boundaries

Ruka wanted my arms
to cradle her beneath my chin,
to wear her like a scarf
but she's possessed.
Who knows how many purrs
before she stops, tail angry,
mouth open and growling
as she side-eyes me
to smack my face and bite my cheek.
She can't be trusted.
She's not allowed.
But look at that face, the sad meow.
Ok demon up you go.

Entryway

It's cute when it's young, the earth
with its tiny shoots of glowing green,
fragile buds, timid reaching branches.
It fills me with relief after winter
abandons its censorship of colors, sounds.
Like the first time in a month
my abdomen twists and shows me
a spot of blight as bright as the season's first leaves.
It's a shorter timespan—
periods feel unmanageable
after a day; it takes spring a month or more
to become an oppressive jungle, once-shy stalks
groping, angry, and waxy leaves trapping humidity
thick with ennui. We can say we're giving up,
we can pretend we have any control,
but nobody is ever convinced.

* * *

A goldfinch is back
four days after I took up a spade
and decided to be serious
about the earth I steward.
I want to believe he's here
for the new,
unbloomed container garden,
but my husband is injured
and the dandelions are seeding.

Orange tabby deep in dreams—
the doorbell rings.
She growls.

Family Resemblance

The cats have devised the perfect layout
of comfortable positions
to pin me in, like stones on tent corners,
or candles marking the points of a pentagram,
securing their belongings against my disaster—
nightmares, needing to pee, getting up
at all, really. At first it was a miracle:
no attacks.
But now they're hedonists,
sleeping in
when once they would beg for breakfast.

I can't reach to turn off the alarm.
Smothered by kin and kit.

Sometimes Fate Requires Two Hands

The star and death.
I can't remember which called first
but it was a tie
when I went to flip them
and laughed.
They're equal today,
transformation and hope.
No despair in total change,
no optimism without radical adjustment.
It's a fair balance
but not enough
in these roiling times.

Gift of the Birch

To make a lash,
wait for the wind—to work,
it must experience its own
unconsenting break,
from heights too far to climb.
A gift for our nature,
like a flower pulled from its bed.

Bring it with you.

It costs a tithe we already pay.

Worn smooth from rough play,
you said you thought
the fallen bark was some
dead animal,
downy gray fur.

Chipmunks and grackles:
we see one of every twelve.
Hungry families hide.

Birds Hate Mondays Too

The sparrow hits the siding, there,
flock watching from the oak.
It clears its head and flies away
as swift as rising smoke.
What's left behind—a memory
more lasting that a mark—
its reputation now as fool,
the dumbest one, a lark.

Queen Tempest

All is hers, every box,
every spot, every hair tie,
every sock,
nothing exists that isn't for her pleasure.
She lies in wait, she sprawls
across the couch, her exposed belly
a treasure and a trap—
we choose to rub it anyway.
We have the tooth-shaped scars to prove
we're fearless in the face of fluff.
She cleans her ear, self-satisfied
and smug. She rules us here.
We bow and scrape
the litterbox clean, her loyal humans,
so eager and so dumb.

Fourteen sparrows dig,
seeds spilled into the soft dirt—
blackbird cracks a whip.

Why Science When I Can Astrology?

I slept last night like the sick do,
an hour or two at a time, not restless—
I feel the rest I took, but interrupted.
These quarantine dreams are vivid
and cut straight to the point.
My subconscious lost the art of subtlety
but developed sudden knowledge
of which sign the moon is in—
Why am I restless? I ask myself,
and answer, *The moon is in Libra now.*

Lessons After Death

All that was left of the mourning dove
was feathers, matted into a loose quilt
scattered like dandelion seeds every rough breeze.
For days I wander thinking *Death is, death is…*
the daguerreotype of Emily Dickinson appearing,
elbow resting, in a snowfall of down.
Finally I shout, *Death is the thing with feathers*!
And smile stupidly. An easy mistake,
this year,
to confuse
Death for Hope.

* * *

Today is gentle,
a little rain, the sun diffused.
I brought them inside
when I put on the perfume
that smells like fresh dirt.
My plants agreed
and exhaled.

Today is soft,
a texture I couldn't imagine
wanting twenty years ago,
like romance novels,
which is most of my reading now.

It took too long to temper myself.
I had to be crushed
before I could prefer the silk
to the stone,
before I learned to breathe
for the joy of it,
a butter sky, a wildflower wreath,
fingertips pressed into dough
instead of bruises.

Snowing pear blossoms
ease us into summer,
hot wind at our backs.

For another year
the only thing I lost
was a good night's sleep.

The First Aid Kit is Missing

The best medicine
dulls the spiky spines of worry,
transforming it from a sea anemone
into a white dandelion. The stalks
of thought remain,
but no longer prick.

I've yet to find the best medicine.

Sanctuary in Wood, in Paper

The attic walls are moss green,
soft, like my earthen heart
mirrored in the sun shafts
of dust motes and the smell
of noon-warmed wooden floors.
Modern house-sounds absent—
electric hum, chiming clocks,
fatal whirring of a computer;
just the wood, creaking
like a pirate ship, and muffled birds
in trees close enough
to caress the house in a storm.
I'll take down the musty books
and travel all day, open the cedar closet
and push through the rough coats
till I find a lamppost in winter.

The seasons turned. I felt the pop
like the top twisted off a glass bottle
and salivated for cooler days
just moments from my lips.

Doctor Boone

He jumps atop me with a mournful call
and guards my soul—my furry paperweight.
A paw across my lips—nothing escapes.
He needs to feel my rising chest, its fall,
a gentle rocking. Face to face. The gall
to sniff my breath, then flinch. The scent abates
and he begins—as ritual dictates—
to knead and knead. It's out of his control.
His vigil doesn't end when he gets bored:
he answers to a higher power. Food?
Attention? Pets? The promise of some treats?
An instinct to protect his human horde?
He soothes me, still, no matter what my mood,
the feline reason that my heart still beats.

Leaves flip light-side-up
before a storm. My turned back.
My silver silence.

One Reason to Befriend Animals

That peach sherbert dawn,
the bane of snore-tired spouses,
birds soft, soft in the expanding light.
They call the sun, the other animals.
They gather for me an army
unafraid and sleepy, ready to stalk,
pounce, play, destroy,
in an orange sky growing white.

Two Scouts

Their eyebrows make question marks,
two little racoons approaching, questioning,
reaching out an ink-dipped hand
to feel my heat-soaked human skin
and sniff and lick the salt
dripping down from above my knees.
They kneel and squat, five fingers
testing shoestrings, sweeping under socks
to check for treats, for shiny, for tasty.
None? They stop exploring
and look imploringly as deep into my eyes
as any lover and ask me, on this sudden day,
why no shiny or tasty.

Giant, velvet slug:
a black cat curls and uncurls
in the afternoon sun.

Echo's purr is a growl.
(The other cats pace.)
Every exhale a warning.

Theme Song Changes Suddenly

All those times I told myself to just move on,
was I listening to the war drums
always beating in the background,
the constant battle-ready rhythm
I mistake for my heart,
and have since youth?

Or have I seen the wave
on its way to my tender home,
and ridden it out and let it go,
to find a new peace?

Not every ripple is a metaphor.
Some are just memories,
some water.

Tea leaves whisper my fate:
soggy and slightly stained.
Ask coffee grounds next.

When the Only Sounds are Birds, Everything Becomes a Bird

A hollow staccato,
somewhere in this low neighborhood—
I hear it echoing in misdirection,
bounced against close, siding-sided walls.
A woodpecker—I look, birds
the only new things in this still-shut home,
but my birds are the same six starlings
and a robin. A sharp beeping and
up farther, two streets over, a truck backs up,
my smile slides down. No bird, then,
but whatever machine hammers together a new house
that animals will find refuge from
in my yard.

* * *

Moths are so polite
when asking for an invitation inside,
like vampires, charming creatures
irresistible when they choose,
when it's impossible to take what they want
by force. Gentle tap against glass,
they need comfort too
and ask for it,
ask me to forget all the times
they assaulted me in public
chased me through twilit backyards
snuck in through cracks or doors
held open a moment too long.
And maybe it would be fine.
Maybe they'd just stay by the light.
Maybe they really believe they can honor
their promises, but I can't risk it.
I can't play frog to their scorpion.
Again. They're terrifying and belong
outside.
They're the number one reason
I built these walls in the first place.

At the Bottom

Descent.
My nose fills with gray,
thick air silt kicked up, settling.
Ground cover for crimes.
We sneak and shift, we lift
the easy targets as we pass,
or plan an intricate demise.
We didn't make the world,
but must survive.

Adapt amidst the grime,
the choking fog, lack of light,
we try to rise.
But everything we've stolen
weighs enough to stop our flight.

Society Turns Me Away and I'm Back to Playing in the Dirt

Under stones, under earth, they coil
in whispers and I can feel each one
as I call, gently, like waking a child.
I hear they're a top phobia.
They've always been, to men,
ever since one bro wrote a story
about how a snake ruined paradise:
one of the earliest examples
of denying culpability, pointing fingers.
He whines that all he ever wanted was to stay
in his exclusive palace, as king, beautiful prize
by his side, everything else locked neatly out.

Men fear women who wield weapons
that look so much like their own
but whisper secrets for hours,
knowledge and knowledge,
where man's only ever says "fuck."
Ignorance keeps us cowed,
and snakes have always been our allies.
I coax them, ask favors.
They're not used to being asked,
only summoned, and then only for dark purposes.
I want to be allies again,
feed them mice, protect them from lawnmowers
and children's boots, and in return
understand
what they've always tried to tell us.

The World Ended While My Neighbor Mowed His Lawn

The birds hopped in the peanuts and asked
monosyllabic what what where
but not about the breaking news breaking
so many times a day for so many days
it became a tide,
it became abuse, a beating,
each wave eroding
our foundations. Of faith, democracy,
my stubborn non-compliance.
My voice was hoarse immediately so I wrote.
Not very long ago, I used my mind
to ponder string theory and poetry.
I could grow—
in that expanse between anxieties—
vast fields of questions,
ploughed and trimmed,
into mazes of ideas.

But today, right now, soldiers of alarm flood the trenches,
wash over me, suffocating, and I must die
because I haven't died yet
and thought I would every day of every month
since 2016
but this must not be the end,
mushroom cloud unfolding against the new sky
what what where
Tom pushes the mower
it drowns me out as I scream
and survive and wait
in that small, terrible mind field
for the next bomb to drop.

It Is Too Goddamn Hot

Air hasn't moved in four days.
I think about getting more bird feeders,
attracting more birds, making them fat, making them
attractive to hawks that will circle our yard
lower and lower, broad wings breaking
the solid atmosphere into a breeze.
I know it'd take more than one hawk.
Power of a fan should be hawkpower.
Today's a 250-hawkpower day.
Besides, more bird feeders mean entering that soup.
It's how I imagine a solid pool of gelatin to really feel—
sticky, hot, inescapable and suffocating.
Smells bacon and sweat stuck in your nose,
on your skin, a sick film,
trying to take a bath after rolling in mud.

Another day and I quit.

* * *

Increase the heat:
we're ready now.
Our steady evolution
marks us for death,
but not before everything else dies.
We learned to practice,
progress in increments
until the impossible becomes the inevitable
and we choke on our own success.

What was the moral of the story?

Or were we ever just a match—
brief and bright,
we devour
even after our extinction.

Evolution Through Excision

If violence has an end,
nobody told us about it.
Imagining a future of peace
feels as difficult and hokey
as 1970's sci-fi, with cat aliens
and planets full of naked women.
Destruction is part of our potential,
and I wouldn't mind if it were deleted,
but I'd have to know beforehand
that everyone understood it meant
we would no longer be human.

A Surprising Case of Self-Protection

My calm is lost
amidst this clawing, desperate scrabble
of irrelevant white men—
so soft, so fragile their feelings,
like blind white slugs writhing helpless.

I no longer hear men's voices:
an improvement. Now to restrain
all their other powers.

* * *

We were always going to destroy ourselves.
This is the dark seed of truth
that drives heroes insane.
They shout for balance while wiping out
any darkness, like extinguishing a candle
with a firehose.

I know it's hard.

You find that grain of sand
embedded in your psyche
and want to dig it out—
Instead, you worry over it and it grows
layer of thin layer of your fears
and insecurities,
and you've just gone and made it bigger.

Most of us leave it alone
or ignore it or deny it,
when others nurse it,
comfort it and feed it.

We fear it's a switch and not a footnote,
like someone could just turn it on,

like that someone is ourselves.

Ambition but Unknown

If I dive in, I'll never get out—
my body vibrates with a hundred things to do
and the fear I'll forget even one.

The coffee packaging said decaf.

But it's too early to stop.
I'm too present to daydream.

I wish someone depended
on me to do something
I'm good at
besides
feed the cats.

Trust Folly

Over the edge
we throw our bones again and again
like we're not fragile,
folly keeping us alive,
if fractured.
But life is in our animation,
the choice to jump,
the fall,
the consequences.
Remove one and we'll be safe—
rusted, and afraid.
I'll keep them and remain
the Fool.

The Climate Changed but I Can't

The door of August shuts,
and I expect the new space to be different,
brittle leaves and fireplace atmosphere immediately,
but the ice cream truck rolls by again
like yesterday, like summer,
its folksy warble rising in waves
like the heat from its metal hood.

I need a better demarcation.

The numbers in the date are approximate
compared to the ones in the thermometer.

I have a right to be cold

and September only provides it in my memories.

Supplanter

I didn't hurry back
from the berry branches and noon sun,
shadow tight against my feet,
afraid it'll shrink and disappear
and not understanding it never will,
that it's physically impossible, that
even in the dark it only expands.

The grackles laugh to themselves, poke
ugly holes into the day, but they don't stay,
they fill with finches and mockingbirds
like snow in footprints, spackle.

My Alarm Clock is the Kind That Wakes You Up with a Gradual Dawning and Nature Sounds

Daylight crawls drunk to my window,
periwinkle and spinning,
trying to be sneaky and quiet
but giggling with birdsong the whole way.
He wriggles in, breathy laughs and stumbling,
shushing himself, pink and glowing with the effort,
until he passes out on the floor, snoring like a jet engine,
and I'm awake for the day.

Voting Isn't Enough. I Have to [REDACTED]

We'll take care of it, they said,
then locked us in
as we watched through the windows
what they meant to do.
Which was nothing.
They laughed to each other
and rifled through what was ours
and gave it to their friends,
and waffled about,
before turning to us and saying
it's safe now.

When they open the door
they'll let death in.

Grackles

I open the walls to let in the birds
and they just snap at me, blue and black
and iridescent like fish gone bad.
Where are the sparrows and finches that sing?
Today's birdsong is a chorus of coughs.
I'd shut them out again but I need the breeze too,
enough to suffer their rough abuse.

Chasing Mourning Doves

I invited them to get too fat,
now they'd rather hobble across the backyard
instead of fly. Or maybe they saw
their brother get caught last summer,
when the hawk chased him into the porch window
and perched protectively on his body,
confused its prey just dropped from the sky,
but wary of competition all the same.
Maybe they can hide in the grass and burrow—
fear can do that to a bird.

Inside Again

My core is a red jawbreaker,
hidden like the chocolate candy buried
in the tip of an ice cream cone.
A molten tide can't erode it—only time,
my favorite measurement, immeasurable
and mystical as each of us.
I'll make you see each layer, witness
the part of me you strip away to see what's underneath.
The joke's on you. It's only layers.
No prize inside, a decoder ring, a memory,
a golden tone.
An answer.
You could have just asked.

* * *

The seasons are lost to me.
How funny, I thought them melted
into one in California, just variations
of hot weather. And here in the heartland,
I get snow and downpours, naked trees,
humidity like shackles—here I live
only a glance at the weather, deciding shoes,
but there's no echo of nature in me.
No planning and planting, no surprises.
Taming wilderness is simple: only forget.

Empires Fall

Trees feel the ferocity of our dominion,
the conquering race chopping a straight path.
Because our eyes are set forward instead,
not like a rabbit or fly drinking the full tour
of possibilities before flight. Machete cuts
too clean, we need a blunter tool, one to splinter
in case we're questioned, one to delineate
our cause, if not effect. What's in our way
will fall or suffer, then forget us
when we finish digging our graves.

* * *

This is not a poem.
You looked for one, and found this,
and I'm sorry.

But I didn't write one today.

I took my delight
and instead of transforming it
into a gift for you,
my selfish mouth swallowed it.

You can't reach it.

I didn't want to share.

Silence is a Lie

Will you shut yourself in your house
will you hear the electricity
will you hear the floors stretch their tight bodies
in relief,
creak and sigh

Will you go to the woods
will you hear the birds and shuffle
of snouts in fallen leaves

Will you be alone
will you shut out the worlds
from your basement or bunker
or isolation chamber

gentle human,
your heart beats.

Every one of you reading this poem
or hearing my words—

your heart is loud.

Bitter Fruit

Portrait of fools,
we had eaten the berries
in dull jewel tones, eaten
until nothing remained
and there was no store of seeds
to make us more.
The best we could do was wait
and search through our own excrement
to find the beginnings of our salvation.

We had eaten all the middles and ends.
Now all that was left to us were starts.
Now all we would know is hunger.

Halloween 2020

I've read the data and know the date
is Samhain, I've noticed the days closing early
and feeding the cats in the dark.
It worries me I haven't felt it yet,
the nearness of a world beyond, veil fragile
and soft—I could turn quickly enough
to glimpse it in corners, in the most insubstantial shadow.

This world has already adapted too much,
much too fast for my soul to catch up.
These past few weeks, if weeks is right
(time has abandoned me),
I've felt my self fracturing, breaking apart gently
and slowly, like the brittle sheen on a still pond.
Memories ribbon free of me and fade and I forget
why they were important once.

I can't recognize the thinness of the veil between worlds
because I'm spread thinner.
I'm hemorrhaging soul.
Scorpio sun, Taurus blue moon, backwards messenger
converging at the hour when one year twists
and becomes another—
there's something vital there. I'm supposed to act
but I can't remember.
I can't remember if I'm supposed to enter
to stay, or to visit,
or perhaps I've been prepared instead
this year
this terrible year
for the great unknowable
to enter me.

More Like "Daylight LOSING Time"

We lose it every year like clockwork.
No wonder we're always off
balance. No other
unit of measurement shifts
like that, our footing steady
in miles.
It is a mystery swallowed by birds in the night
and repeated at dawn
for our uncomprehending ears.
I can't imagine time
beyond my position to the sun:
a winter afternoon—it is day,
it is cold.
Why make a difficult concept more nebulous?
Why impose a tide on a river?
In at one equinox, out at the other.
The skunk still sleeps. The cardinal wakes.
I peel the numbers off the clock
but it is not enough.

Before the Birds Awake

It's a comfort to sit in the dark,
to cast in the corner that frightens me,
and be the monster.
The writing is unknown,
I know it's mine but the letters
shift, too deep in a shadow
for the late-coming dawn,
the icy gray of driving to work
in the struggling, early light.
But I don't worry about that now.
I've transformed
for a while. My landscape
is waking up on the wrong side of the sun
and waiting while the day opens.
What poets saw this same sky,
the same silence of a pre-industrial morning?
From my forgotten corner, I hear no heat, no horns—
no mean lights of progress
to illuminate my gaze into this past.

Witness

Our history unravels like dropped measuring tape,
yarn across the floor,
banners of our demands
unfurling over bannisters.
The horror pins us on a board,
hovering limbs slowly pinwheeling,
uncomprehending.
We know the answers
we ask anyway—
ask why they tell you that you cannot,
invoke enough spite to can.
Ask what your life as a woman is worth,
then worship its seditious inversion.
Ask who owns, who seeks, who needs,
as we're put in a corner to seethe.
The world needs less
of everything but us.
Run the big men out.
Our eyes inescapable.
Our mouths untrained.

Selenite

It's a shock
to be again as flawless
as fallen snow—
impressions of paws
and boots and hooves
and claws
eaten up.

How certain are you of your absolution?

You're just one prayer away,
but I have a disc of polished white
that removes all trace of use.

A crystal sin eater,

the envied goal of men and church.

Forced factory reset,
and virginity restored.

Tell Them I'm Fine

I'm the one to cut and run,
to find closure and progress
in the swiftness, seamless, thoughtless
running. More away than toward,
but please don't tell. Don't tell
you've seen me soft, don't tell
I feel, am human, am lost.

I always lose this game.

Be a dear, a friend, my voice—
tell them I'm fine.

The Season of Murder Mysteries

A wicked pool, stamped in time
with twigs and sticky shadows—autumn left
and didn't tell anyone. Not the snow,
the shroud of winter, covering the dead
for months, for each moment, for ever.
Seasons will shift
from hope to hidden horror,
from rot to denial to surprise.
We like the landscape, the big picture
of inhaling hills puffed up with colors,
eye tumbling orange, blood-red, bruise.
It's only weeks later we disdain
what turned beautiful and glowing—
like we don't know
beatitude precedes the steep valley slope to death,
don't know the leaves
nest maggots and mice bones.
We do.
We just like it tucked in out of sight,
like to imagine beneath the blanket growing
crocus, not corpses.

The Shrinking Forest

The hills are brittle with leafless trunks,
exposing dull-colored soldiers wandering
like there's no war, like they were once fierce
and ready for a fight but weeks of walking,
of canned food and no fire, no enemy,
eroded all their sharp reasons to march and shoot
and left them bare.
Overcast.
One day they'll amble
right back to their front doors and wonder
when the world got muted.

I Only Have One Regret but Holding It Is A Full-Time Job

Nobody expects the long reach of time
to come slinking, grabbing
out of the murky plasm of the past,
to slide up your body and grasp your collar
while you watch paralyzed,
this slow-motion disaster
of remembering something
you never wanted to remember.
It's too late to rectify, by years,
by decades, but its grip keeps turning,
turning your head back to it
like you were supposed to have learned something,
grown to a place where you look upon it
and nod sagely and feel nothing.

I know of no one who has been able to do this.

It must not be possible. Nostalgia
must be unkind, or that grip
on my chin is my own hand
tense with disappointment
and the desire to spread it.

Ok.

Ok.

I'll watch again, you wretched wraith.

* * *

Is this our winter now?
How it will go?
The ceiling fan has stopped, the daylight late,
me awake and waiting, marking time
with nowhere else to be. I hate
uncertainty. What a boring thing to say.
Am I just boring now, locked away
behind a winter, and a war, a plague?
Yet in this season is the faintest
seed of spring,
a slitted eye hiding in the dawn,
a star to keep me company at night.

* * *

I kept my soul in a pocket watch.
Broken, but ticking, the second-hand shudders,
a constant second-long cycle—
hope, attempt, fail, cry—
it breaks my heart.
Like seeing any bloodied bird
and not knowing how to help.
I could take it to be fixed,
but who to trust? Precise, work,
a wisdom, at what cost?
I know the sound now, familiar
with what comes next.
I can be convinced I'm happy.

Bold of Me to Buy a Planner for the Upcoming Year

What does it matter that we open
new calendars, that we collectively agree
to call the next twelve months 2021?
We've been weighing time like this for millennia,
and for the past ten years have uttered, hopeful,
Maybe Next Year Will Be Better.

It isn't.

Men drew boxes around days and a line
in the damn middle of winter as if blindfolded
and struck out with a pointed finger.

The earth knows better.
The earth knows.

Our hard lines are her gradients
and you know how much men hate that.
They want to fall asleep one night and awake
with the sun and say *now everything's changed.*

It's so easy. It's a lie.

A turned page doesn't turn the tide.

Our hearts in the earth do that.

The Heart

Such fragile walls
to hold a pulsing thunder,
shouldn't it split?
Shouldn't it tear
like tissue paper, ebbing
tones forced
again against, a beat.
Another.
I throw myself
as recklessly, consistently,
to any open heart, crushed
and crushing, bouncing back,
even hurt and breathless.
What else never rests?
What else means death
upon its ceasing? Love
in its increasing? I've increased,
I'm full and drunk
and feeling every pulse,
its wake a pause before another plunge.
I hold my breath.
I press.
I jump.

Resolutions for the New Year

Last night of the year and the wind is a gentle chorus
of chanting monks—
polite noise
to get my attention.

Maybe I'll learn their song
this time.

I know how it looks.

The branches are carved and polished
like warm knives,
whole trees of them caressed by cold sound.
I wish I were a guerrilla knitter for all these trees,
but there are forests full
and the needles carved and polished
like warm knives
only fit in my two hands,
and I never learned how to knit.
Only how to listen.

Maybe It'll End After All

This isn't the light of a landlocked dawn.
I crouch beside the window
and look up, beads of frozen rain
pixelated on the screen,
and beyond is that periwinkle gray sky
of one hungover morning in Revere.
The ocean just too far to hear,
echoed in the traffic driving through slush.
I forgot my toothbrush
and underwear and went home
sticky and dry
and sleepless. It wasn't so cold for a coat.
I think of it often, mostly my eyes all gritty,
the feel of yesterday's clothes—worn so long
they were becoming a part of me—and
the idea that though nothing had changed,
somehow I was a new person.
A tired, dehydrated person, but new.

Winter At Last

Snow would fall, our guesses
fragile as each flake—
how it'll stick, how high,
the sound and texture of our thrice-socked,
rubber-booted feet
as we ran across the smooth paths
of what we should have shoveled.
We hid in snow forts—literal forts,
dug out of towering mounds,
with tunnels and slides.
I disbelieve it now—
piles never get so high,
my body never was that small
and light, where I could alight
over the crust, tunnel beneath,
without collapse. An isolation chamber,
packed walls of the fortress
muffling, quiet gray fall
a gentle blindfold.
The past has lost its edges,
its wilds hidden
for the next stumbling children.

About the Author

Jacquelyn Merrill Ruiz was raised in New England, forged in Los Angeles, and embraced by Cincinnati. She's written all manner of genres for years, but it was her poetry that earned her the coveted Master of Professional Writing at University of Southern California. She currently lives in Ohio, where she toasts the full moon with kombucha and gathers thunderheads for later use.

Find out more about the author online at
www.jmerrillruiz.com

www.ingramcontent.com/pod-product-compliance
Lightning Source LLC
Chambersburg PA
CBHW020939090426
42736CB00010B/1201